Titanic S

The Story of Harold Bride

Paul Shipton

Contents

OXFORD
UNIVERSITY PRESS

OXFORD
UNIVERSITY PRESS

Great Clarendon Street, Oxford OX2 6DP

Oxford University Press is a department of the University of Oxford.
It furthers the University's objective of excellence in research, scholarship, and education by publishing worldwide in

Oxford New York

Auckland Cape Town Dar es Salaam Hong Kong Karachi
Kuala Lumpur Madrid Melbourne Mexico City Nairobi
New Delhi Shanghai Taipei Toronto

With offices in

Argentina Austria Brazil Chile Czech Republic France Greece
Guatemala Hungary Italy Japan Poland Portugal Singapore
South Korea Switzerland Thailand Turkey Ukraine Vietnam

First published 2003

British Library Cataloguing in Publication Data

Data available

ISBN: 978-0-19-919542-8

20 19 18 17 16 15 14 13 12

True Stories Pack 2 (one of each title) ISBN: 978-0-19-919545-9
True Stories Pack 2 Class Pack (six of each title) ISBN: 978-0-19-919544-2

Acknowledgements

The publisher would like to thank the following for permission to reproduce photographs:

Corbis/Bettmann: p 14; Corbis/Hulton Deutsch Collection: p 31;
Corbis/Ralph White: p 3; Mary Evans Picture Library: pp 8, 22;
Marconi: p 7; Ulster Folk Museum: p 5

Front cover background artwork : Kay Dixey
Inset photo: Marconi
Back cover: Ulster Folk Museum

Illustrations are by Kay Dixey

Printed in China by Imago

Introduction

In 1912 more and more people wanted to cross the **Atlantic Ocean** from England to the United States of America. The *Titanic* was the biggest and most famous ship built to make this trip.

When Harold Bride joined the ship on its first voyage, his job was to work in the radio room. He didn't know that he would play a part in one of the worst disasters at sea the world had ever seen.

The *Titanic* being built

Chapter 1

"Queen of the Seas"

People have called me a hero. I don't know about that, because there were many heroes in the early hours of 15th April 1912.

I was only 21 that year. I had worked for nearly a year as a ship's radio operator.

In April I started a new job – on the *Titanic.*

My first sight of the ship, in Belfast, took my breath away. Now I understood why people called it the "Queen of the Seas". The *Titanic* was the biggest … and the best.

Passengers boarded the *Titanic* in Southampton on 10th April. At noon the great ship set off on its voyage to New York.

The *Titanic* docked in Belfast

For first-class passengers the *Titanic* was like a wonderful floating hotel with fancy restaurants, a library, and even a swimming pool.

There were lots of other passengers, too. Many had one-way tickets, looking for a new life in America. Of course, these people weren't allowed near the higher **decks** of first class.

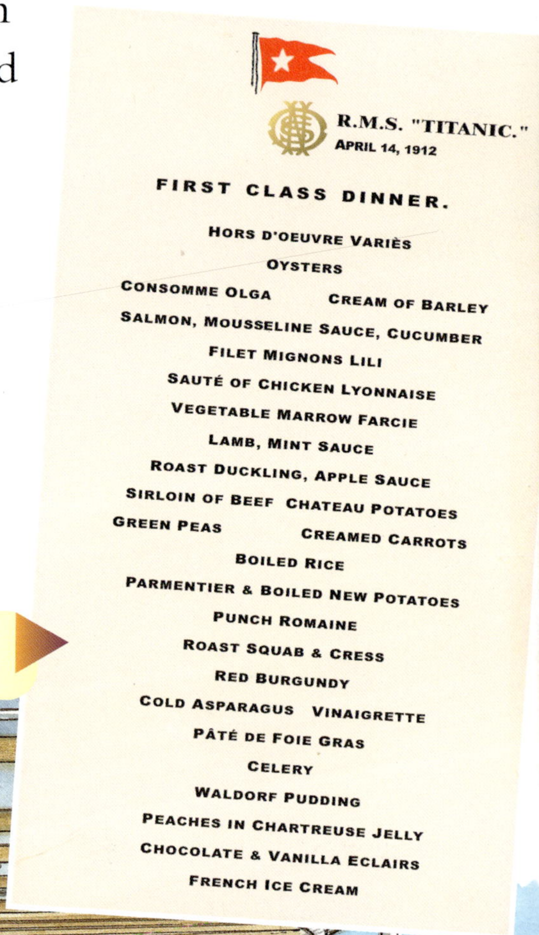

R.M.S. "TITANIC."
APRIL 14, 1912

FIRST CLASS DINNER.

HORS D'OEUVRE VARIÈS
OYSTERS
CONSOMME OLGA CREAM OF BARLEY
SALMON, MOUSSELINE SAUCE, CUCUMBER
FILET MIGNONS LILI
SAUTÉ OF CHICKEN LYONNAISE
VEGETABLE MARROW FARCIE
LAMB, MINT SAUCE
ROAST DUCKLING, APPLE SAUCE
SIRLOIN OF BEEF CHATEAU POTATOES
GREEN PEAS CREAMED CARROTS
BOILED RICE
PARMENTIER & BOILED NEW POTATOES
PUNCH ROMAINE
ROAST SQUAB & CRESS
RED BURGUNDY
COLD ASPARAGUS VINAIGRETTE
PÂTÉ DE FOIE GRAS
CELERY
WALDORF PUDDING
PEACHES IN CHARTREUSE JELLY
CHOCOLATE & VANILLA ECLAIRS
FRENCH ICE CREAM

A first-class menu

Harold Bride

Jack Phillips was the Senior Radio Operator. He and I had to send lots of messages from rich passengers. We tapped these out in Morse Code. Sometimes it was hard to catch the messages that came back.

Jack and I quickly became good friends. That was lucky, because we lived and slept in the radio cabin!

Chapter 2

Iceberg!

We were especially busy on Sunday, 14th April and it was a long, hard day for Phillips.

We received a few warnings from ships about ice ahead. Captain Smith knew about these, but he wasn't worried – not on the "unsinkable" *Titanic.*

Phillips had so many messages to send from passengers that he even interrupted one ice warning.

I was supposed to start work late that night, so I went to bed early in the evening. I was asleep when the accident happened. I didn't feel anything.

Around midnight I got up and asked Phillips how everything was.

"I think the ship's damaged," he told me.

Minutes later, Captain Smith appeared. "We've struck an **iceberg**," he said.

The captain returned a few minutes later. He told us the ship was sinking.

"Send the call for assistance," he said grimly.

"Yes, at once!" answered Phillips. He began sending out the ship's position and a message for help in **Morse Code**.

It was hard to believe. The "unsinkable ship" was going to sink.

We weren't worried yet.

"You'll see your first iceberg," Phillips joked.

Several ships replied to us, but they were all too far away.

As Phillips looked for a closer ship, I ran to the **bridge** with messages. The crew had begun to load passengers into the lifeboats. Women and children were supposed to leave first.

At first, some passengers refused to go. "How could the *Titanic* sink?" they thought.

So many people couldn't believe what was happening that some of the first lifeboats were almost empty. But slowly people understood the danger and there was no problem filling the lifeboats.

Children cried as their parents put them in the boats. Husbands and wives kissed for the last time.

Finally, a ship called the *Carpathia* replied to our radio call. It was coming to help.

We continued looking for other ships and Captain Smith asked what message we were using. Phillips told him it was "CQD" – "Come quick, danger."

I suggested using the new Morse Code signal for help, which was "**SOS**". We joked that we were sending the first ever SOS from a sinking ship.

Chapter 3

The Terrible Truth

The joking stopped when we worked out how long the *Carpathia* would take. It would be here in four hours, but the *Titanic* would sink in less than two. No one could rescue us in time.

Phillips searched for closer ships and I ran to and from the bridge with news. The decks were steeper now as the front of the ship sank. Some passengers prepared themselves for the end.

Other passengers tried to fight their way onto the remaining lifeboats. How many of them knew the terrible truth? There had been more than 2,200 passengers and crew on the ship, but there were only enough lifeboats for 1,178! It became more and more difficult for the ship's officers to keep order on the decks.

Back in the radio room, I put an overcoat around Phillips' shoulders and tied a lifebelt round him. It was getting much harder to send and receive messages now because the power was weak. Water was getting into the engine rooms.

The noise from the decks was terrible. I don't know how Phillips continued to work.

The captain came to the radio cabin one last time. "You have done your duty," he told us. "You can do no more. Now it's every man for himself."

The water had reached the deck outside our cabin, but still Phillips did not leave the wireless. He continued sending more and more messages.

I went into one of the other rooms for a minute. When I looked out, I saw a man from the engine rooms behind Phillips. The radio operator was too busy to notice him, but the man was trying to steal his lifebelt!

I charged out angrily. Together Phillips and I fought the man off.

Finally, with water pouring in, we abandoned the cabin. Phillips and I said goodbye. It was the last time I saw my friend alive.

The deck was very steep now, but the ship's band were still playing!

Some people were trying to free the last lifeboat. I ran and began to help them.

Chapter 4

The End of the Titanic

The ship sank lower and suddenly a huge wave rolled up the deck towards us. It swept the boat, still upside-down, right off the ship. I grabbed hold of a **rowlock** and was pulled with it. The next thing I knew, everything was dark and I was plunged into the icy water.

I was inside the lifeboat, but the lifeboat was upside-down! I struggled for air as the freezing water of the Atlantic splashed me. I didn't know it, but more than 20 people were above me, on top of the boat. Finally, somehow, I managed to dive out from under the lifeboat.

Hundreds of people were in the water all around me. Their cries were terrible.

I looked back at the remains of the ship. It was sticking right up out of the sea. It looked like a duck diving under the water.

Incredibly, the band still played!

Members of the band

I began to swim with all my strength. I was afraid I might be sucked down along with the ship when it sank. The ship's lights went out in its last few minutes.

My fears of being pulled down went away as the last of the great ship disappeared slowly under the water. At 2.20 a.m. the *Titanic* was gone.

I was very cold and tired by now. Luckily, there was a boat near to me. It was the upside-down lifeboat – the same one I had been trapped under. I was pulled up out of the water.

But we weren't safe yet. There were too many people on the boat and it was losing air. We were slowly sinking.

An officer on the lifeboat, Charles Lightoller, shouted instructions and everyone had to move so that the water didn't sink us. Everyone except me ... My legs hurt so much that I couldn't move them. We prayed and waited for dawn.

Chapter 5

Lights in the Distance

The *Carpathia* still hadn't arrived. Where was it?

Luckily, another lifeboat saved us. Even though it was already full, they let all of us on board. It was in this boat that I finally saw lights in the distance. It was the *Carpathia*!

It was a long slow job picking up all the survivors. At last the people in my lifeboat climbed the rope ladder, one by one, onto the *Carpathia*. My feet hurt terribly as I climbed up, but at the top, hands reached out to help me. That's when I passed out.

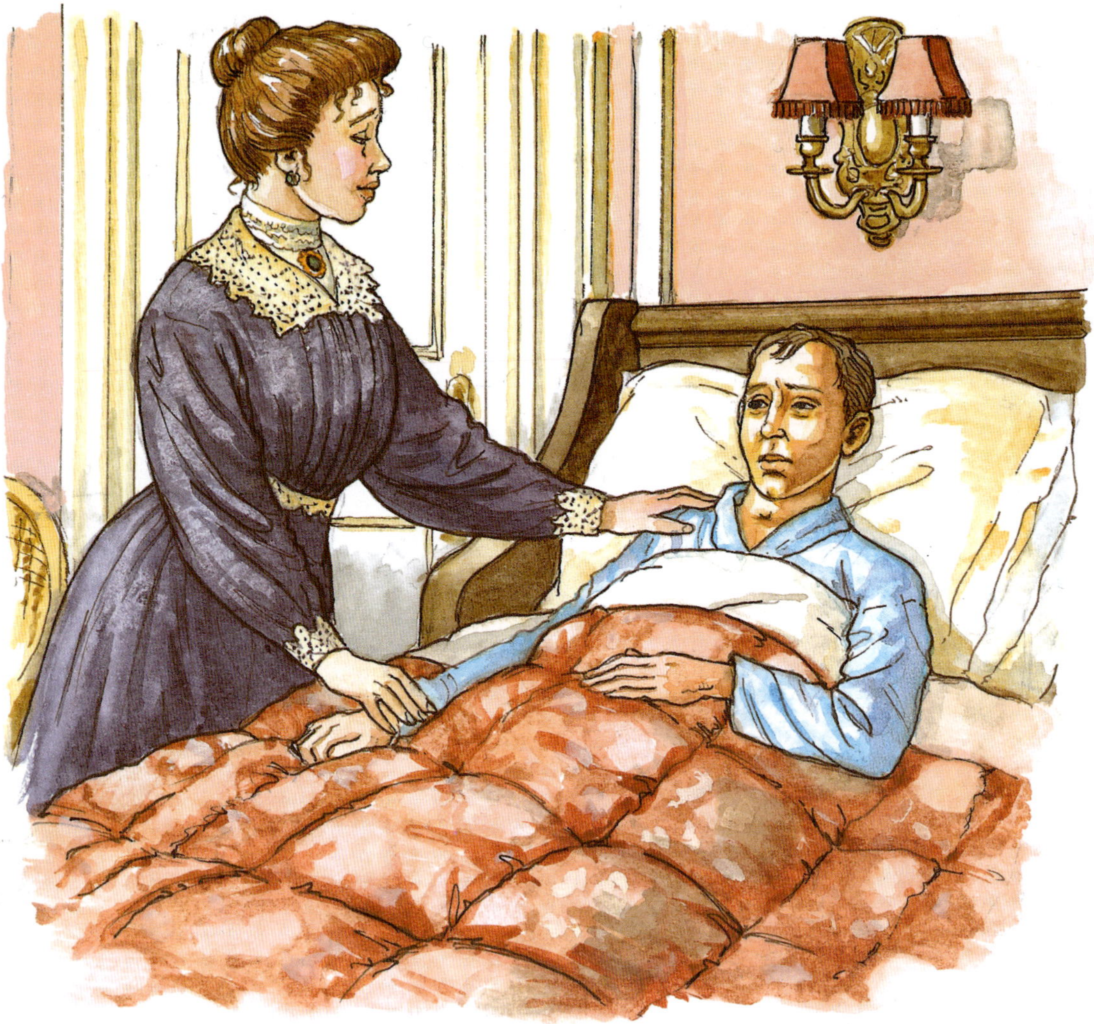

I woke up in a room on the *Carpathia*. I had survived the most terrible disaster at sea the world had ever seen. But I could not be happy. Many others were less lucky than me. My good friend Jack Phillips had lost his life.

Although my legs were injured, I knew that the radio operator on the *Carpathia* needed help. People on land were eager for news of their loved ones. Who had survived? Who had not?

I spent the rest of the trip to New York in the radio room, sending messages to passengers' families and friends on land.

Years later, what I remember most about that terrible night are the acts of bravery. I remember the band playing until the very end. And I remember Jack Phillips staying at the wireless. In my mind, he was the hero who saved us all.

Harold Bride lived for more than 40 years after the night the Titanic *sank.*

Glossary

Atlantic Ocean the second largest ocean in the world. Ships travelling between England and America must cross the Atlantic Ocean.

bridge the part of a ship from which the captain controls the ship

deck a level on a ship that people can walk on. The *Titanic* had nine decks.

iceberg a large chunk of ice floating in the sea

Morse Code a system for sending and receiving messages by tapping out dots and dashes. At the time, a ship's radio operator had to use Morse Code to send and receive messages.

rowlock the part of a rowing boat where the oar is attached

SOS a signal calling for help

Timeline

1912

April 10th ***Noon***
Titanic leaves Southampton

April 14th ***11.40p.m.***
Titanic hits iceberg

April 15th ***Midnight***
Captain Smith and builder inspect damage

April 15th ***12.05a.m.***
The captain gives order to prepare lifeboats

April 15th ***12.10a.m.***
The captain asks Phillips and Bride to call for help

April 15th ***2.20a.m.***
Titanic finally sinks

April 15th ***Dawn***
Carpathia arrives at the scene of the disaster

April 18th ***Evening***
Carpathia arrives in New York with survivors

Index